Home Loans. Mortgage for veterans and militaries

GRIN Publishing

Bibliographic information published by the German National Library:

The German National Library lists this publication in the National Bibliography; detailed bibliographic data are available on the Internet at http://dnb.dnb.de .

Imprint:

Copyright © 2014 GRIN Verlag GmbH
Print and binding: Books on Demand GmbH, Norderstedt Germany
ISBN: 978-3-656-84536-2

This book at GRIN:

http://www.grin.com/en/e-book/284074/home-loans-mortgage-for-veterans-and-militaries

GRIN - Your knowledge has value

Since its foundation in 1998, GRIN has specialized in publishing academic texts by students, college teachers and other academics as e-book and printed book. The website www.grin.com is an ideal platform for presenting term papers, final papers, scientific essays, dissertations and specialist books.

Visit us on the internet:

http://www.grin.com/

http://www.facebook.com/grincom

http://www.twitter.com/grin_com

Buy or Refinance a Home without down Payments

Are you are veteran? Are you worried of where you can get refinancing to get the home of your dreams? Well, worry no more. VA loan is the appropriate package for any veteran and military. It is tailored to ensure that cater for VA mortgage Loan as well as Military VA loans. The better part about the loan is that, the repayment is very much friendly. The rates are all low; the terms are favorable to all those who desire it, and lastly, zero down payment.

0$ DOWN PAYMENT UP TO THE VA LIMIT

Never say die! It is now clear that Veterans and Military can have a life that they desire. They can live in homes of choice and locations of their choice. This is courtesy to the program that is well made to take care of their needs. The VA mortgage loans and the military VA loans requires 0$ down payment. What much better would be realizable? They enjoy benefits that cannot be advanced to any other ordinary citizen from any financial institution. Default of pay or lack of pay is next to impossible for them because the repayment is fair and tailored to meet their financial muscles.

Important to note though, not all of the veterans are qualified to get the VA home loans. The veterans have to meet the criteria set forth by the department of Veterans and then they get issued with it upon cutting then minimum threshold. Upon qualifying, the loan is issued by private lenders. The requirements of the loan are as elaborates below. The veterans and the military should avail the following:

1. The residential address for the place they have lived for the past two years
2. The employers and their addresses for the past two years of their work
3. Their social security number
4. The gross payments supported with W2 and recent check stabs for the past two years
5. All the account numbers that they hold and the specific banks with the proper details of the exact names, monthly payments and monthly repayments.
6. Those who have their own business will need to proof compliance to taxation by offering tax returns, current income statement and finally the balance sheet of the company.
7. Finally, all those who own a property and would wish to benefit of this loan, after application they are to get the property appraised and pay for credit report.

Types

As always, are available to ensure that you enjoy every bit of getting a loan. May it be the Veteran VA mortgage loan, VA home loan, military VA loan? It is best that the decision you make will not be worthy regrets in days to come. That is our ultimate joy. Never worry that it's your first time, we know that you deserve information to be at par with those with knowledge.

Crucial to note is the considerations made before issuing the loan. It is therefore imperative that all those who wish to apply know so that, they do not get offended after realizing they are not qualified at late stages. Those who qualify are the military personnel who have served for a period of not less than 90 days during a time of war, or a period of not less than 181 days during a peaceful period or not less than six years as a National Guard. Those who served in the peaceful period, the days given previously are to be continuous service without any break.

The law indicates that for the veterans to qualify, they should have served the military at least for two years if you joined after 7 September 1980. It is likewise for an officer who begun work after October 16, 1981.

Guidelines to follow:

1. The debt-income-ratios are the best solutions for military and veterans who wish to obtain news homes. They should make calculations to know what VA loan mortgage they can manage.
2. Finally, it is important to note that, the loan may not be approved. It is therefore advisable that the ones who desire to have house seek preapproval; before looking for one. Once it is approved, it gives them assurance and confidence while looking for the home of their choice. It is also best for those who sell. They get the assurance that the buyers are serious with the offer and that they mean their word.

Debt Ratios

It is a directive that before a loan is issued the debt ratio of either the applicant or that of the spouse is able to meet the expenses associated with owning a home.

PAYMENT

The payment of the debt is fixed and it is compared against income which is said to be effective. The debt ratio which is acceptable for that particular case is equal or less than 41%.It is however important to note that there are exceptional conditions which allow an individual with a debt ratio of more than this percentage to be accorded an opportunity. The calculations are done on the basis of adding up the total mortgage payment (principal and interest, escrow deposits for taxes, hazard insurance, homeowners' dues, etc.) and all recurring monthly revolving and installment debt (car loans, personal loans, student loans, credit cards, etc.). Then, take that amount and divide it by the gross monthly income.

VA Refinance Loans

This is a loan program me which has been tailored to finance those people who previously had another form of financing. It can be opted for because of various reasons. Firstly, it can be an option of consolidating other forms of financing which are expensive to service. Secondly, it can be a means of financing funding education. Thirdly, it can be as a result of making improvements in a home. Finally, it can be used for other purposes that are well highlighted at VAloan.com. It is made to have different categories from which a choice is made. The following are the available choices:

- VA Cash-out Refinance Loans
- Interest Rate Reduction Refinance Loans
- Streamline Refinance Loans

VA Cash-out Refinance Loans

This is the first option. The re-financing is done to Veterans and military who own homes. It is usually valid for those of them who aspire to own their own private residences. The good thing with either of the loan is that it does not require the owner of the home to have lived in it for a given period of time, or for them to have had a loan for a given period of time. The major requirement is that the home which is used to refinance is equally fit in the equity to refinance. The loan is usually refinanced up to 100% of the appraised home amount. The amount in question for refinancing can include the closing costs if they will be covered within the appraised amount.

Interest Rate Reduction Refinance Loans

This is the second option of refinancing which is open to those who were servicing their previous loans subject to eligibility requirements. This is a loan that is clearly meant to for lowering the rates that are previously being serviced. That is the concept of reducing the amount of money which will be paid at the end of the day. It is also a strategy which is used to ensure that the repayment being made periodically is minimal compared to the one the owner of the home is currently servicing.

VA Streamline Refinance Program

Under this is where the interest rate reduction refinance loans were realized. This is where those who previously service a VA mortgage are able to reduce the interest rate without getting into their pockets. That is the reason it is also known as streamline refinance or a VA to VA loan.

The essentials of VA stream line Loan

1. It is notable that once the deal goes through, there are no refunds.
2. Assumptions are forbidden
3. Unlike other forms of finance, there is no need for appraisal or any type of report is it the termite report or credit report. The mortgage though should have been paid as agreed in the past 12 months and must be up to date at the date of financing.
4. If there is any lien, it should be subordinate to VA loan.
5. The loan gives a provision to include all other costs to the new loan to avoid getting money out of personal pocket. The interest rate is made with that particular concept in consideration.

VA Loan Program

Fixed VA Loan Repayment System

This is accredited to be one of the best ways for owning a dream especially for those who are employed. The better part of it is that they are able to do the calculations of the debt-income ratios in order to know the option which is best for them. The option which is best for them is the one which allows for them to be in a position to cater for the expenses that keep rising.

Truth is told; selling or buying a dream home can be difficult for an employee. Would you imagine saving for more than 20 years to get the home of choice. That is a long period! Not only that, it is next to impossible to save for that long because, idle money will never meet emergencies and get used up. The best part of the VA mortgages for the Veterans and Military is that they are extended for years regarding the mortgage and them agreement that is reached at by the client and the private lender.

The fixed form of repayment becomes the best because; the owner of the loan will know the exact amount that they will part with at the end of each agreed fixed date in the long duration up to 30 or more years depending on nature of the agreement. That way, it is possible to budget for income and live in a dream house as early or as young as one wishes.

The use of ratios in determining what kind of a dream house an individual wishes to live in is a financial requirement which is meant to ensure that the family to the veteran lives well even after acquiring the home. This is not the only criterion which is set in determining who qualifies for the loan. There are other things which are always observed. They include the credibility and credit worth history of the individual in need of a loan.

A summary of what is needed to qualify for the VA Loan

- The credit history should be clean.
- The history of credit should show that you used the money well and in the right way.
- To have the lowest possible debts from other avenues.
- Ensure that you are employed permanently or for the long run.
- Have liquid assets or the assets which equated to ready cash.
- Should have enjoyed the benefits of the military.

Partnership in bettering the debt-Income-Ratio

It is imperative to note that a partner is the one who can be legally indentified. As to whether one can use a person they are aspiring to marry in days to come as their co-borrower? That can never work. There is no legal evidence that the two are partners or if they will ever be in the future. This case is much applicable between a man and a lady. Either of them may be a veteran and may not qualify to get a loan. Some think to get their future wife and husband to cover them, but that is totally impossible. It is not until they are married and have the evidence of the marriage certificates can they use such a procedure.

However, there is an exception to all this. The exception indicates that, if at all the loan has to be issued to the veteran; it has to be limited to the interest the total amount or property of which s/he owns.

Are the benefits of the Veterans enjoyable by either the Children or their spouses on their absence?

It is imperative to note that, the benefits that were not enjoyed by a veteran cannot be enjoyed by the children under whatever circumstances. There are no debates about that, because that is how it has been. The veteran may likely not be available because of death or going missing on the online of work or duty. The spouses too are not allowed; though there are different circumstances which allow them to enjoy the benefits. The following are the exemptions:

1. If the veteran died as a result of service or related factors.
2. If the Veteran when missing in Action for a period when in line of duty
3. Finally, if the veteran a prisoner of war for 90 or more days

VA ARM (Adjustable Rate Mortgage)

What about it?

Just like loans, VA ARM is loan in form of a mortgage which has a lifetime which is agreed between the parties involved. This is the mortgage that is preferred by most of the veterans who want to have their homes of dreams financed. They love it because it is fair enough to consider their plight in increasing or minimizing the interest rate of payment on a yearly basis.

Further, it is also good to know that ARM has two branches. The very first branch is traditional adjustable rate mortgage. This is the most common. The interest rate can go to a maximum of 1% in year and a maximum of 5% on it lifetime. The adjustment is usually applicable after the first one year because a fixed rate is usually applied on the mortgage initially.

There are millions of advantages to using this option of ARM. The most central of all the advantages is that it reduces the cost of operation. The cost is usually brought down because the veterans are able to negotiate on the closing costs so that they are brought down as much as possible. It is also important to note is that the veteran can negotiate the interest rate of payment with the lender. Well, it is also fine to note that, it is not compulsory for those who own such kinds of loans to pay monthly insurance premiums. The better part of the mortgage type is that there are no penalties for delayed payment. What a better offer would anyone be in need of!

The above said type of ARM loan is usually guaranteed by the Veterans administration. So is the second type of loan which is known as the hybrid ARM loan. This is at some point similar to the traditional ARM. They have differences though. The major is that, traditional can take up to 2 years only while hybrid can take five or more years. The rate is usually limited to 1% in the case that the years are five of less. The rate is fixed to 2% if it covers a period of five or more years.

It has its advantages as well, even though they are much similar to those of traditional. The first advantage is that it does do not give an option of down payment. This is a relief to the veterans who are qualified. Just like the traditional VA home loans it is the same for hybrid because the amounts of cost they can pay as closing costs are limited. It is also good to note that the veterans department has not in any time advertised the insurance for such mortgages. To make matters better, it is helpful to note that those who are members of this mortgage have the discretion to make payments just as those who own traditional ARM. Such discretion ensures that they do not pay penalties for the lateness or default that they may have at a given point.

It is categorical to note that traditional VA ARMS and hybrid VA ARMS guaranteed by the VA do have a 30 year repayment plan. This is in line with the terms which are properly stipulated in their case. They do also have a1 year warranty and 10 year protection program for new house buyers.

Making decisions which are not informed can be a lot much costly in the long run if not in the short run. It is thus advisable to factor various things before falling for either traditional ARM or hybrid ARM. The cost of initial mortgage payment and the lifetime rate of the rate increase of the loan. The choice should not be informed by a matter of thinking this is what I think is best. It has to be informed on such calculations in order the end results are enjoyed to the maximum.

It is never good that you live a life of stress. Stress will only make you thin and die young never to enjoy the benefits of the VA home loan. In that case it is best that you talk to the officer discharging the loan to help you plan by advising you on how to utilize either of the adjustable loans. That is the only way that you will be able to enjoy the services of the loan to an extend of 39 years without having to worry. It is wise too to note that even after getting projections from the officer in charge, which may not be the same case in real way.

VA Loan History

VA home loan has its origin trace back to 1944. It was known as the servicemen's Readjustment Act or (the GI Bill of Right). It contributed to the betterment of the livelihoods of the people of America. It also made the economy of America to improve just after the bill was signed into an active law by the then president Frank D. Roosevelt. The families of the veterans were able to get houses of their dreams at a tender age without any down payment. This is the law that opened many other doors of loans for the veterans. This has become a pillar of hope for more than 29million veterans as well as the service providers who are not in a place to build or buy a house of choice at a go.

The VA loan is to be granted to any of the Veterans who have served for a period of less than two years since September 7 1980 and for officers who served from October 16 1981. For the other veterans, they should have served at least 90 days during war time or 181 continuous days during a peaceful period in order to qualify for the VA home loan. Without any of the aforementioned qualifications no VA can be afforded to any of them. It is quite different for reservists or the National guards. For any of them to qualify for the loan they have to ensure that they have served for a period of not less than 6 years.

As earlier on elaborated, it is impossible for the children of a deceased veteran tot enjoy any of the benefits that they were entitled to. That is not the same case for the spouses. There are guidelines which dictate the qualifications of a spouse of a veteran. They can only enjoy 25% benefit of the total benefits that were to be enjoyed by the veteran. But, this is only applicable if the spouse veteran died or went missing for 90 days in service, duty or service related issues. The veterans are usually entitled for a lump sum VA home loan of $417,000 but the spouse can only get $104,250.

The limits which the veterans can get as home loan are usually set by the department of Veterans, and it is specific for each particular county in the US. The veterans are able to get a loan based on the appraised amount of the property that they own or the purchasing price plus 2.15% VA funding fee for the first time use of the loan. For the reservists, they are entitled to 2.40% of VA funding of the loan.

Veteran Affairs (VA) guaranteed loans are usually issued by many of private lenders. The private lenders are able to issue the loans to the veterans because of the guarantee from the veteran department that in case they fail to pay, they are entitled to 25% of the total amount. That is the reason why the rates by the private lenders are favorable. The VA home loan is meant to purchase a single housing unit of up to bedroom which can house a family. The house has to be proven to be used for the personal use. In that particular case, it should not be bought for letting to other members of the public. The private lenders giving the VA mortgages include the credit unions, savings and loans, banks and finally the mortgage companies for the veterans of the US. Any of the veterans who wish to get a loan to buy a home can approach any of the private lenders. Though, it is good to have met the predetermined threshold.

VA Closing costs

The veteran pay can be to the maximum for the customary or it reasonable amounts for the Items fees and charges which can either be for one or all. On top of it a charge of 1% constant rate has to be charged by the private lenders. The provisions are not similar in the case of construction, repair or maintenance. The provisions for this category are known as the as special.

All charges and Itemized fees

It worth noting the department of Veterans takes good care of them. It defines what the veterans are supposed to pay as fees and charges. It also gives the closing costs which are to be paid by the borrower of the loan. All other costs are dumped to be the work of the seller of the home or the lender of the loan. They are to take care of those extra costs. The costs are said to be reasonable and customary to each specific VA loan office.

All items being mentioned are as highlighted below:

1. The recording fees
2. Appraisal and Compliance inspection
3. Credit report
4. Survey
5. Flood zone examination
6. Title examination and title insurance

7. VA funding fee (unless exempt from the fee with a 10% minimum disability from the VA)

8. Prepaid items, including a portion of taxes, assessments, and similar items for the current year chargeable to the veteran and the initial deposit for the tax and insurance account.

9. Hazard insurance: The veteran can pay for the hazard insurance premium. This includes flood insurance, if required.

The veteran is not to pay for all charges. There are some charges that they are not allowed to make. They are known as the non allowable" Itemized fees and charges". They are as highlighted below:-

Document preparation, loan closing or settlement, attorney services for anything other than title work, preparing loan papers for conveyance fees, locking in interest rate services, photographs, stationery, mailing or postage charges, telephone calls, amortization schedules, general overhead, membership, escrow charges or fees, document preparation and / or assignment, notary, loan application, processing, loan broker or finder's fee other than your mortgage company, trustee's fees or charges and tax service.

When negotiating a real estate contract, it is wise to review allowable borrower fees and charges. Many items can be paid for by the seller of the home and can be negotiable when presenting an offer on a home to the seller. We strongly suggest that you utilize the services of a real estate professional and consult with your real estate professional when handling the transaction.

Debt Ratios for VA loans

It is very well that before a veteran gets the VA Mortgage they meet the office to calculate for them the ratios. There are specific ratios which have been predetermined by VA to help the home owners to be in a position to cater for the costs and expenses that come with home ownership. It is bad to get a home and lose it or live in it without any peace of mind. Hence the idea of VA to ensure that the veterans can only get a home of which they can manage the expenses that come with owning it.

How to calculate the effectiveness of the Loans repayment based on Income

Add up the total mortgage payment (principal and interest, escrow deposits for taxes, hazard insurance, homeowners' dues, etc.) and all recurring monthly revolving and installment debt (car loans, personal loans, student loans, credit cards, etc.). Then, take that amount and divide it by the gross monthly income. The maximum ratio to qualify is 41%. In the event the number exceeds the 41%, the VA has a residual income guideline which can allow approval, yet are not considered a compensating factor.

Saving Money for Veterans

It is categorical that the VA funding fee of 2.15% is dictated by the law. That is for the case that the loan does not require a down payment. This is thought of because of reducing the burden to the tax to the tax payers. When they pay the fee, they contribute towards the benefit that they enjoy. Important to note too is that for the second time borrowing of the VA home loan by the veteran, the fee funding goes up to 3.3%. This is the same case; the Veterans do not have to make an initial down payment. The increased fee for funding is meant because; the Veterans are thought to have enjoyed the benefit once unlike others who have not had the chance. It is also assumed that ever since they got the first benefit, they have been able to save and accumulate some good chunk of money.

It is not always that no down payments can be made. There is an option of for down payment in order to bring down the fee required. For all the military members who desire to get loans for purchasing homes, for construction or for repair, they are to pay based on the fee set by the VA. It elaborates that for the members who make a down payment of not less than 5% and not more than 10%, then they have to make a payment of a fee of 1.5%. For those who make a down payment of more than 10%, they have to pay a fee of 1.25. For those who do not make a down payment at all, they are required to pay a fee of 2. 15%. For second time users, those who do not make any down payment, they are entitled to a fee of 3.3%. For those who make a down payment of more than 5% but less than 10%, they have to make a payment of 1.5%. Lastly is those who make a down payment of more than m10%, they have to pay a fee of 1.25%. This is an indication that there is more advantage to make a down payment when applying for this kind of loans.

For those who are in the other category of reserves/National Guard they are to pay a fee of 2.4% in the first time in the case that they do not make a down payment. In the case that a down payment of less than 10% but greater than 5% is made, a percentage of 1.75% is applied. When the down payment is more than 10% then, the percentage is a slow as 1.5%.for the second time, when a down payment is not made, the fee goes up to 3.3% while with a down payment of more than 5% and less than 10%, a fee of 1.75% is applied. In the case that a down payment of more than 10% is made, then the fee is all down at 1.5%.

In conclusion, it is valid to summarize that regular military can pay a fee of 2.15 for in the case of cash-out refinance loans when they do not make down payments. They are entitled for an incremental fee the second time of application. The fee comes to a constant of 3.3% the subsequent time after the first in the case there is no down payment. For the National Guards/ Reserves the rate is 2.4% in the case that they do not make down payment when it is their first time. They have to pay 3.3% when it is the second time and there is no down payment. Down payment of more than 5% and less than 10% entitles first time veteran to pay a fee of 1.75 and the second time to make a payment of 1.5%. The same rates are applicable in the case that the down payment is more than 10%.It is different case for the Interest rate reduction loans which have a VA funding fee of .50 and 1.0% on manufactured Home loans.

There are specific people who are exempted from paying the funding fee. They are as highlights below:-

- The veterans who are being compensated because of the fact that they got a disability while in service.

- The persons who did not get retirement pay yet they are entitled for disability benefits that they become party to during their service years.

- Finally is the spouses to the veterans who died as a result of disabilities which might have been as a result of the service that they tirelessly rendered to the country. It does not matter whether the spouses themselves are members of the veterans too. It does not matter too whether the spouses are using the entitlement of their spouses who passed on or that of theirs.

In conclusion, it is wise to note that all in all, VA has the final say and will know who to exempt and who not to.

Credit Issues for VA Loans

VA is categorical that, the veterans who have a clean repayment history for the past 12 months are likely to make repayments in future. The clean record includes timely submission of the payments. The other side of the coin is applicable in accordance to them.

ON TIME VS. LATE PAYMENTS

When a veteran or veteran and a spouse pays their VA loans within 12 months after the date of last derogatory credit it is said to be on time but any payment after 12 month is considered as late payment and does not weigh in the borrower's favor. The VA automatic underwriter analyzes borrower's credit but actually they do not put into consideration the whole picture .for example the period of slow payment during financial difficulty does not disqualify the borrower if a good payment pattern has been maintained since then with proper description. Any account that have been reduced to judgment by a court of law must be either paid in full or subject to a repayment plan with a history of timely payments on that plan.

NO CREDIT OR HISTORY AT ALL

Lack of an established credit history should not prevent one from accessing a particular loan as provided in the VA credit standards that if person in need of loan has a satisfactory payment history like rent, phone bill ,utilities etc may be used to check his/her viability to loan.

BANKRAPTCY - CHAPTER 7 (Total Liquidation)

A veteran must have a minimum of 2 years that elapses since the day he /she was declared bankrupt in chapter 7. The borrower must have re-established good credit, qualify financially and have excellent long-term employment.

BANKRUPTCY - CHAPTER 13

In this chapter VA will consider a borrower still paying on chapter 13 bankrupt if he is verified for a period of one year, the court trustee will need to give approval to proceed. The VA will require veteran to write a full explanation of bankruptcy. The borrower must also have re-established good credit, qualify financially and have excellent long-term employment.

JUDGEMENTS, FEDERAL DEBTS AND COLLECTIONS

If the collection is determined as minor in nature, the underwriter can usually waive the need for the debt to be paid off as a condition for loan approval. If a borrower is in any debt he /she won't be viable for the loan. Federal loan include student loan, tax liens.

FORECLOSURE

Any veteran borrower whose previous residence or other real estate property was foreclosed on or given a deed-in-lieu of foreclosure within the previous two years since the disposition date is generally not eligible for a VA insured mortgage. If the foreclosure was on a VA loan, the applicant may not have full entitlement available for the new loan.

CONSUMER CREDIT COUNSELING or CCCS PLAN

If a veteran, or veteran and spouse, are participating in a Consumer Credit Counseling Plan because they have prior adverse credit, the underwriter may determine them to be a satisfactory credit risk if they can demonstrate 12 months' satisfactory payments and the counseling agency approves the new credit.

VA Loans and Occupancy Law

Living in the VA Funded Home
VA loan requires borrower to certify in writing that they intended to personally occupy the property as their home. Veteran must; personally live in the physical property as their home, intend upon completion of the home loan within 60 days after the loan closing. This applies to all types of VA loan except for interest Rate Refinancing Loans.

Co-signors & Joint VA Loans

Getting more out of your VA loan

The VA guidelines recognize legally married spouses of qualified veterans as co-signors on VA loans and can include their income. These loans can be fully guaranteed by the VA.

The VA guidelines will allow for more than one eligible veteran(s) to purchase a home. If more than one eligible veteran is involved, VA divides the entitlement charge equally between them, if possible. These loans can be fully guaranteed by the VA.

While the VA guidelines may allow for a non-veteran to co-sign for a mortgage loan, they will not fully guarantee the loan. The VA Guarantee is limited to that portion of the loan allocated to the veteran's interest in the property. That means the VA will not fully guarantee this type of loan and our company cannot originate loans that are not fully guaranteed by the VA.

Loan Calculations

Five Easy Steps to a VA Loan

The VA loan process is not any much different from taking a mortgage. It is very similar to the other procedures followed when taking other types of loans. The only difference is that for a veteran to get the loan they have to issue out a certificate to indicate that they are eligible of the program. The other bit is that the interest rate is usually very low compared to other mortgages with the opening of not giving down payment.

The loan can easily be processed by the veteran and very fast based on the appraisal they receive from the appraiser. They may decide to go by the review they get from them instead of waiting for the VA. The process is known as the VAs' Lender Appraisal Processing Program (LAPP).

What to do:

1. The first step is to apply for eligibility certificate for those who do not have. They are to fill form VA Form 26-1880 and present it to any eligibility centers. The form should be accompanied by papers showing that they have been active military members in regards to the period after September 16, 1980.
2. The second step is identifying the house to buy.
3. The third step is to determine the worth of the home, what is known as an appraisal. This can be achieved through reaching the VA office. This is mostly undertaken by the lender.
4. The veteran is supposed to apply the loan as the appraisal is taking place to any of the lenders. The lenders will seek credit information of the applicant. The lenders can proceed if they are granted the permission to do automatic processing upon the receipt of VA or LAPP; they can proceed to closing the application. In the special case where the loan is not to be closed without the approval of the VA office, the Veteran will write a letter to it office, and the lender will be informed of its decision.
5. The final step where the loan is closed and normal business resumes.

VA Loans: A GOOD DEAL FOR VETERANS

More than 25.5 million veteran as have used the benefits of VA financing entitled to them. However, they can still use VA refinancing because of they may have their entitlement restored to them or even some remaining benefits. It is better to get a VA home loan other than getting a normal mortgage for a house. The benefits with the Home loan that the veteran should consider include the following:

1. No down payment
2. Loan maximum up to 100% of the property appraisal.
3. Rate negotiation
4. No payment of monthly insurance premium

5. Appraisal which informs the buyer the value of the property
6. A choice of repayment plan
    - Traditional fixed payment
    - Graduated Payment Mortgage
    - Growing Equity Mortgages
7. The construction of a new house is inspected to meet approval plans. The plans should have a warranty. At least a one year warranty is required for the plans, and that is the reason for the inspection. In case the warranty is up to ten years then, only inspection will be done at last to check conformity with accepted plan.
8. The right to repay the loan without any penalties
9. VA does servicing of person loans and gives free guidance to the veterans to avoid their homes from being sold or repaying with difficulties.

Uses for a VA Home Loan

1. To buy a home which is VA approved.
2. To build a new home.
3. To buy and improve a home at the same time
4. To improve an existing home by bettering the features in it.
    -Important to note though, the loan can be taken to as high as $3,000 based on documented costs. It can even go as high as $6,000 as long as the mortgage repayment is offset by expected reduction in utility costs. Refinancing can only be up to 90% of the appraisal plus the additional costs.

5. To refinance and existing VA loan to reduce the interest rate.
6. To buy an already built home.

Who is Eligible for a VA Loan

1. The veterans who were served by their country during the World War II and later period are eligible for the loan. They should have been active during this particular time.
2. National Guard members and reservists who were activated for the period that passed August 2, 1990 and served for the period ended 90 days.
3. Selected members of reserves including the national guards who are not otherwise eligible and have served for a period of 6 years and have been discharged honorably or those who have served for 6 years and are still serving.

Cost of Obtaining a VA Loan

All veterans are expected to pay a funding fee of 2.15% with an exemption of those who chose to make a down payment. Those who make a down [payment of more than 5% but less than 10% are supposed to pay a funding fee of 1.5%.those who make a down payment of more than 10%, they are supposed to pay a funding fee of 1.25%.

For the Reserve/ National Guard individuals, they are to pay a funding rate of 2.40%. The rate is usually less in the case that they make some down payment. For instance, they pay a rate of 1.75% in the case that the down payment is 5% to 10%. In the case that the down payment is more than 10% the funding fee is 1.5%.

FUNDING FEE

A basic funding fee of 2.15 percent must be paid to VA by all but certain exempt veterans. A down payment of 5 percent or more will reduce the fee to 1.5 percent and a 10 percent down payment will reduce it to 1.25 percent.

A funding fee of 2.40 percent must be paid by all eligible Reserve/National Guard individuals. A down payment of 5 percent or more will reduce the fee to 1.75 percent and a 10 percent down payment will reduce it to 1.5 percent

The other funding fee is 3.3% for the veterans or reservists who are enjoying the entitlement a subsequent time after the initial.

The final funding fee is for refinancing an existing VA home loan in order to reduce the interest rate. The funding fee is 0.5%.

EXTRA CLOSING COSTS

There are some extra closing costs which may be brought in by the lenders. This varies with the lenders and the customs and laws in different parts of the country. The costs are either payable by the veteran or the seller. The costs include:

- VA appraisal
- Credit report
- Loan origination fee (usually 1 percent of the loan)
- Discount points
- Title search and title insurance
- Recording fees
- State and/or local transfer taxes, if applicable
- Survey

WHAT MORE TO LEARN ABOUT THE VA LOANS?

Those who desire to get more information on the VA loans, they consult the nearby offices or they can get the VA Pamphlet26-4 or VA Pamphlet 26-6.

The Truth about VA Appraisals

The information about the VA home loans is available online as VA Pamphlet 26-7. It gives a wealth of guidelines on what is expected. Actually it is located in the Department of Veterans website. The information is highlighted step by step what takes place during the appraisal. The appraisal is usually needed because it becomes the security for the loan.

The very first appraisal is usually catered by the borrower. The need of the appraisal is to ensure that the property meets the minimum requirement set forth by the VA. The costs of the appraisal should include the subsequent inspections of checking compliance.

The appraisal is in accordance to the stipulations of chapter 10 indicates that, the lender is the one who is to initiate the appraisal. Even though, it is not locked at that. It is still open to other persons to initiate. In the case that the lender is using mortgage brokers or agents, they should ensure that they are informed of the chapter. What matters is that at last, the appraiser will be approved by the VA.

Before even the process of appraisal request begins, it is advisable that the property meets the criteria of appraisal in accordance to (Sections 10.5 through 10.10). In some other case, the office of the VA can be contacted for help. For instance in the case that the eligibility of the property of not certain; or when the property is not eligible but can be used as the security to the loan.

It is also important to note that it is not essential neither is it possible to request for an appraisal in the case that a property has a value assigned to it by the VA. There are other circumstances which lead to ineligibility of a property they include the following:

- When the party who wants to conduct the appraisal is not allowed doing so by the government.
- When the party is excluded from participating in Loan Guaranty Program because of sanctions as a result of veteran prejudice.